Writing Prompt Advent Calendar

Countdown to Christmas with a writing activity every day for 24 days

by Melissa Gijsbers

©2024 Melissa Gijsbers
melissagijsbers.com

Finish This Book Press

Written by Melissa Gijsbers

Cover Design using elements from Canva

ISBN: 978-0-6489603-9-3

All rights reserved. Apart from any permitted use under the Copyright Act, no part of this book may be reproduced, copied, scanned, stored in a retrieval system, recorded or transmitted in any form or by any means, without the prior permission of the publisher.

Dedication

To all the creative Christmas lovers looking to get in the Christmas spirit with stories.

Table of Contents

Dedication iii

Introduction 1

Melissa's Golden Rules of Writing 3

Tips on how to use Writing Prompts 5

Writing Prompts 7

Conclusion 31

About the Author 33

Also by Melissa Gijsbers: 35

Introduction

Welcome writers,

There are so many ways to count down to Christmas with an advent calendar. You could have a chocolate advent calendar, one with picture books, Bible verses, perfume, tea bags, and so many other options.

Several years ago, I had the idea that a writing prompt advent calendar would be fun, and in 2023, I ran a program with 24 Christmas themed writing prompts that were sent to participants via email.

I have taken some of those prompts, some other Christmas themed prompts I have used in writing groups, and some new ones and put them into this book.

I have included only the writing prompt only as this is not a journal. I don't want you to be limited by the space in this book for your writing. I encourage you to write in the way that suits you, whether it's writing in a notebook, typing on a device, voice to text software, or something else. You could also use these as conversation starters and invite your family to make up stories over the dinner table.

You can use the prompts in order or choose prompts at random. You can also spend as much or as little time writing each day as you wish.

You can also use these prompts again in future years and come up with different stories that are just as fun to write as the first time.

I hope you enjoy these writing prompts, and they bring joy to you this Christmas.

Happy Writing and Merry Christmas!

Melissa Gijsbers

Melissa's Golden Rules of Writing

1. **Have FUN!** - creative writing is all about the process. After all, if you're not having fun, what's the point?

2. **It's YOUR Story**—write your story your way. There is no single way to write a story, so experiment, play, and write whatever comes to mind.

3. **Experiment**—play with different styles and genre. You never know what you'll enjoy writing until you try. Plus, you don't have to limit yourself to just one type of writing.

4. **Try something new**—if your story isn't working, try something new. A different point of view, style, genre, or even a new prompt if the one you're working on isn't working!

5. **Have FUN!** - Did I mention have fun? Whether you

are writing something silly or serious, creating a story is fun, so enjoy it.

6. **Write as long or as short as you like**—If you only have a few minutes, then you can write something short. It doesn't matter if you don't finish a story or piece of writing in a sitting, or at all.

7. **First drafts are meant to be crappy***—this is something many people don't realise, it's no issue if your first draft is not perfect. Everything can be fixed up in the editing process.

8. **You don't have to finish**—if you're writing for fun, and you don't finish your story, that's okay. You can always come back and finish it another time.

9. **Have FUN!** - I may have mentioned this before… have fun writing your story, poem, or whatever else you're writing.

* Crappy = flawed, imperfect, incomplete, not up to scratch, unsatisfactory

Tips on how to use Writing Prompts

1. **Read the prompt carefully**— What is it asking you to do?

2. **Think outside the box**— Is there a way you can use the prompt in a fun or unusual way?

3. **Use the prompt more than once**— If you have more than one idea, then write them down. You can use a prompt in many different ways. You can save them to use next year, or even after Christmas if you get in a story writing mood.

4. **Just write**— Don't worry about titles, spelling, grammar, or anything else, just write. This is a first draft. Underline any words you're not sure about spelling and you can come back to them later. Everything can be fixed up in the editing process.

5. **Read over what you've written**— When you've done, read over what you've written and fix up any obvious errors. Then you can have fun editing your story to share (if you want to).

Writing Prompts

1

You are decorating for Christmas. One of the decorations on the tree comes to life and starts talking to you. What does it say and why?

2

A Christmas card arrives in the mail addressed to you. The handwriting is a beautiful cursive that belongs to another era, and the postmark is from December 100 years ago. Who sent it to you and why?

3

Write a letter from the Elf on the Shelf explaining why they haven't shown up this year

4

Many people send a Christmas newsletter to friends & family. Write your own Christmas newsletter for yourself or a fictional character

5

The last line of your story:

And this is why we never eat leftovers or anything Aunty Joan brings for Christmas dinner.

6

Presents are a big part of Christmas. Write something about either the biggest present you can imagine, or the smallest!

7

Write a story that is not a romance that somehow involves a Christmas decoration.

8

Create a new joke or riddle for the inside of a Christmas bon bon!

9

Write a diary entry from one of Santa's elves. It can be from any day of the year

10

Write a letter to Santa. This could either be from yourself or from a fictional character

11

Write something inspired by a myth or stereotype around Santa Claus that tells the 'truth'

(ie can be completely made up but goes against what people think they know)

12

Write a Christmas story using the following random words:

Book, Vacuum, Table, Window, Necklace

13

Write a story about a disaster in Santa's workshop

14

Write a Christmas wish list for a fictional character, either one you have created or one you love from books, TV or movies

15

You wake up and find yourself in a Christmas movie. Write a story about your experience & how you get back to 'real life'

16

Explain how Santa enters houses that don't have a chimney

17

Choose an unlikely food and come up with a story to explain why it is an essential & traditional part of your family Christmas dinner

18

Rewrite the words to a popular Christmas song or carol for a warm, Australian Christmas

19

It's your end of year Christmas party, and a dragon shows up. Write a story about what happens.

20

Write a story that involves eating Christmas leftovers in some way

21

It's Christmas morning. You run to the tree, but something isn't quite right. What happened & how do you put everything right again?

22

One Christmas, you receive the wrong present. Write a story about what happens

23

Your Christmas cake has a used by date of 23rd December, but you serve it anyway as it looks and smells okay. What happens when people have a piece of Christmas cake on Christmas day?

24

Write a story about Santa's adventures on Christmas Eve... from the point of view of one of the reindeer

Conclusion

I hope you've had fun with this writing prompt advent calendar and enjoyed crafting stories with the writing prompts.

One fantastic thing about writing prompts is that you can use them more than once and come out with an entirely different story. There is no rule to say that you can't write Christmas themed stories at any time of the year!

If you do want to use the prompt again and aren't quite sure what to do, try writing from a different point of view, or a different style or genre than you did last time. You can also put this book away until next year and try them all again with a fresh mind.

Try it and see what happens.

If you want to keep writing, head over to my website and sign up for my free 12 Days of Christmas program. This starts on Christmas Day and goes for 12 days.

Each prompt is related to Christmas, New Year, holidays, and summer (as I'm in Australia and it's our summer holidays).

I hope you have a wonderful Christmas this year.

Happy Writing,

Melissa Gijsbers.

About the Author

Melissa Gijsbers is an author and booklover. Stories have always been a big part of her life, and she has been writing them for as long as she can remember.

She started working with young writers in 2013 at the Monash Public Library and has been inspiring them to write by providing them with crazy writing prompts ever since! This group helped Melissa discover how important creative writing can be for wellbeing, and how much fun writing prompts can be.

Her first book, *Swallow Me, NOW!* was

published in 2014. Since then, she has published more books and written even more stories that may or may not be published.

She currently lives in Gippsland in Victoria, Australia and spends quite a bit of time coming up with fun writing ideas for stories, as well as writing more books herself.

You can find out more about Melissa and her books on her website— www.melissagijsbers.com

Also by Melissa Gijsbers:

- Swallow Me, NOW!
- 3... 2... 1... Done!
- Lizzy's Dragon
- My Princess Wears a Superhero Cape
- My Mummy is Evil
- Genie in my Drink Bottle & other writing prompts
- Great Lost Sock Mystery & other writing prompts
- Creative Writing for Wellbeing
- Writing Prompts – Random Words
- Stories Through the Rainbow short story collection

www.ingramcontent.com/pod-product-compliance
Lightning Source LLC
Chambersburg PA
CBHW072339300426
44109CB00042B/1952